# MAKING SCIENCE WORK

# Flying and Gliding

TERRY JENNINGS

Illustrations by
Peter Smith and
Catherine Ward

RSVP

RAINTREE
STECK-VAUGHN
PUBLISHERS
The Steck-Vaughn Company

Austin, Texas

Published by Raintree Steck-Vaughn Publishers, an imprint of Steck-Vaughn Company

A Mirabel Book

Produced by Cynthia Parzych Publishing, Inc.
648 Broadway, New York, NY 10012

Designed by Arcadia Consultants

Printed and bound in Spain by International Graphic Service

1  2  3  4  5  6  7  8  9  0  pl  99  98  97  96  95

**Library of Congress Cataloging-in-Publication Data**
Jennings, Terry J.
    Flying and gliding / Terry Jennings : illustrations by Peter Smith and Catherine Ward.
        p.   cm. — (Making science work)
    "A Mirabel book."
    Includes index.
    ISBN 0–8172–3959–6
    ISBN 0–8172–4252–X (softcover)
    1. Aeronautics—Juvenile literature.   [1. Aeronautics   2. Flight.]   I. Smith, Peter, 1948– ill.
II. Ward, Catherine. ill.   III. Title.   IV. Series:  Jennings, Terry J.  Making science work.
TL547.J444   1996
629.13—dc20                                                                            95–6001
                                                                                              CIP
                                                                                               AC

**PHOTO CREDITS**
Air France: 28
Boeing Commercial Airplane Group: 5 center
British Aerospace Airbus Ltd.: 24
Cameron Balloons: 4 bottom right, 6
Cessna Aircraft Co.: 5 bottom, 17
Gruman Corporation: 5 second from top
Jennings, Dr. Terry: 20
Museum of Army Flying: 5 top
Super Stock Inc.: 4 top, 7, 29
U.S. Air Force Academy, Colorado: 4 bottom left

Note: The aircraft pictured in this book are not
        all drawn to the same scale.

## Key to Symbols

"See for Yourself" element

Demonstrates the principles of the subject

Warning! Adult help is required

Activity for the child to try

# Contents

# Flying Machines

For thousands of years people have wanted to fly like birds. Some people even attached wings to their arms. Then they jumped off hills and tall buildings and were injured. But people cannot stay in the air by themselves. Our muscles are too weak. Our bodies are too heavy. But there are now many flying machines that can carry people. You can read about some of these aircraft in this book.

Parachute

Glider

Hot air balloon

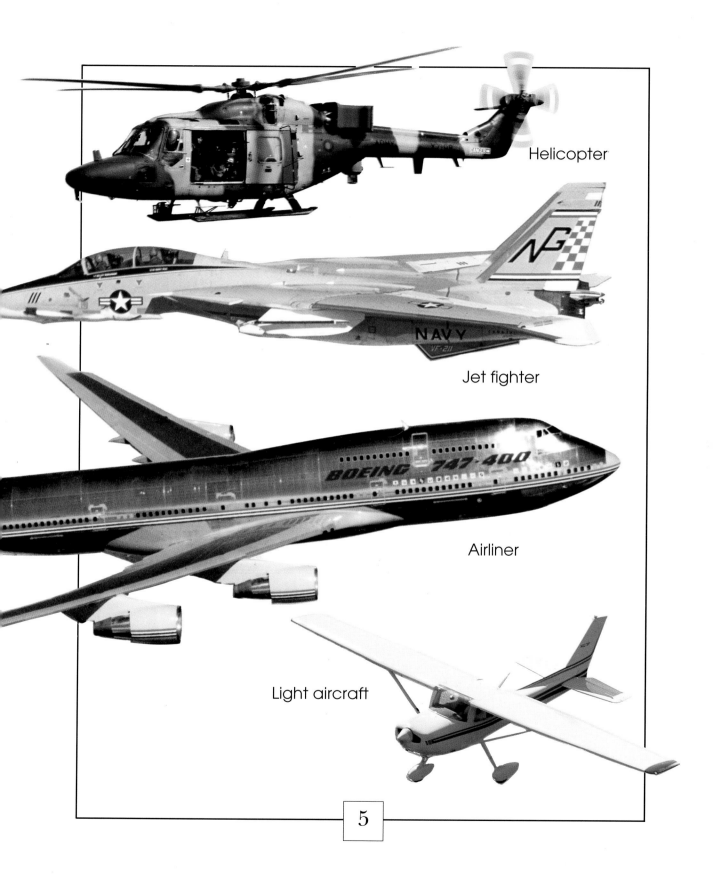

Helicopter

Jet fighter

Airliner

Light aircraft

5

A hot air balloon can fly. The balloon is really a huge bag. It is made of very light cloth. The passengers and pilot stand in a large basket. The pilot turns on a gas flame. The burning gas makes the air hot. The hot air makes the balloon fly.

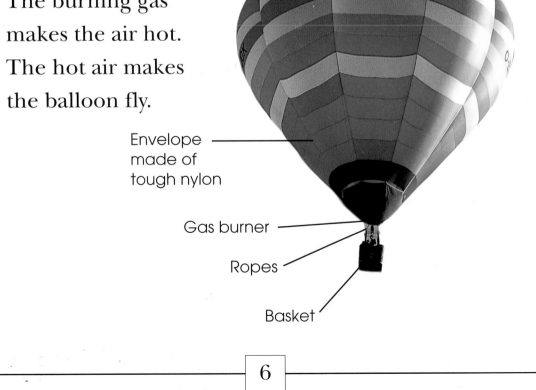

Envelope made of tough nylon

Gas burner

Ropes

Basket

Unlike normal aircraft, hot air balloons do not have wings. They are filled with hot air to lift them off the ground.

# Inside a Hot Air Balloon

The gas flame heats the air inside the balloon. The hot air rises. Hot air rises because it is lighter than cold air. This hot, light air makes the balloon rise and float in the air. The balloon goes where the wind pushes it. To make the balloon come down, the pilot turns the flame off. He or she may also open the hole at the top of the balloon.

Parachute vent

Rip line to parachute vent

Gas burner

Basket

To make the balloon rise, the crew turns on the burner. This heats the air inside the balloon. The hot air spreads out, making it lighter than the cold air outside. If the crew wants the balloon to go down, they open the parachute vent at the top. This lets a little of the hot air out. Heavier cold air flows in, making the balloon sink.

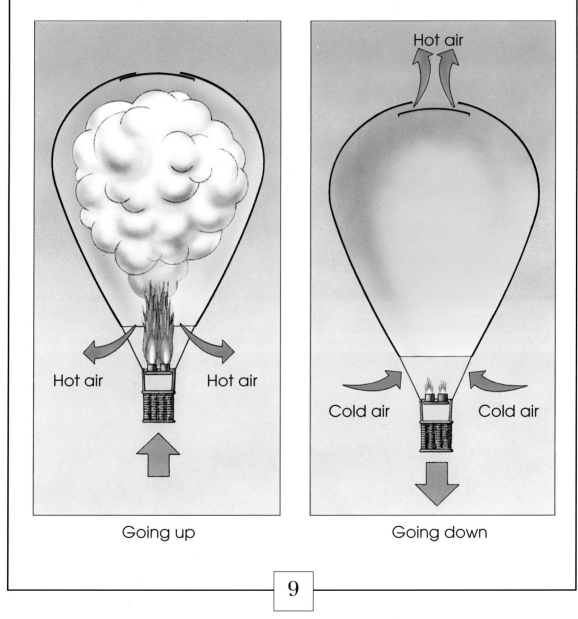

Going up                    Going down

A hot air balloon rises because warm air takes up more room than cold air. Blow up a balloon. Tie the end. Measure around it with a tape measure. Hold the balloon above a hot register for a few minutes. Measure it again. Is your balloon now bigger because the air inside it is warm?

1 Blow up the balloon.

2 Measure the balloon.

3 Hold balloon above a register

Find a plastic bottle. Place a balloon over the mouth. Ask an adult to put the bottle in hot water. See how the balloon gets larger as the air inside it takes up more room.

Balloon

Balloon stands up

Plastic bottle

Dish pan of hot water

A glider is a simple aircraft. It does not have an engine. But it has long, narrow wings to help it soar through the air. Gliders can only get off the ground if they are towed into the air.

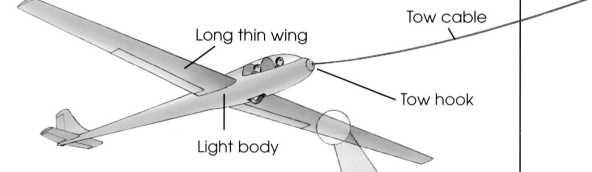

Long thin wing

Tow cable

Tow hook

Light body

Faster air

Slower air

A glider can fly because its wings are a special shape. Each wing is curved more at the top than underneath. This shape is called an airfoil. All aircraft wings are this shape.

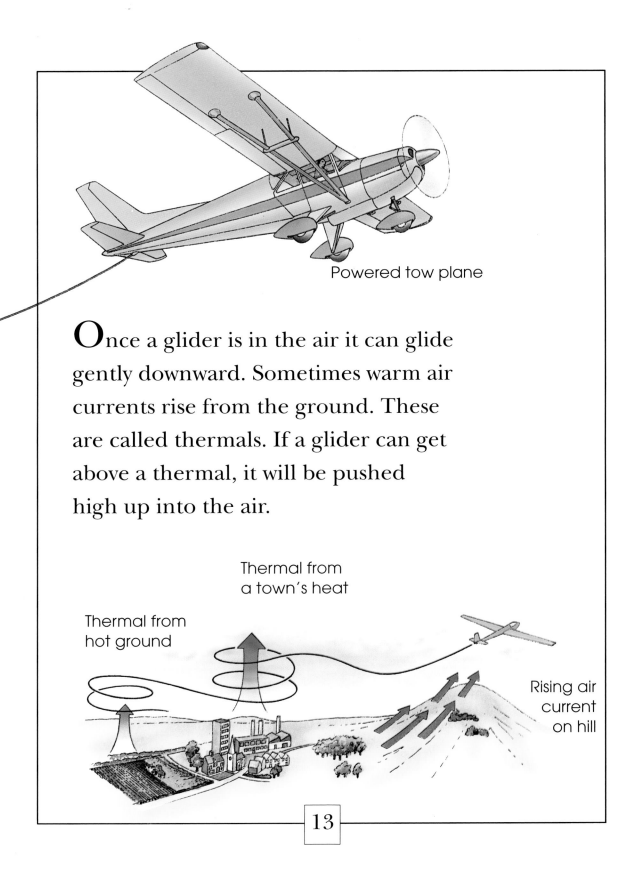

Powered tow plane

Once a glider is in the air it can glide gently downward. Sometimes warm air currents rise from the ground. These are called thermals. If a glider can get above a thermal, it will be pushed high up into the air.

Thermal from a town's heat

Thermal from hot ground

Rising air current on hill

You can see for yourself how an airfoil works. Fold a thin piece of paper into a wing shape. Tape the ends. Then blow hard against the front edge of the wing. The air going over the top of the wing moves faster than the air going underneath it. This makes the wing lift.

Blow hard.

Paper wing moves up.

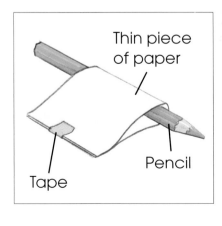

Thin piece of paper

Pencil

Tape

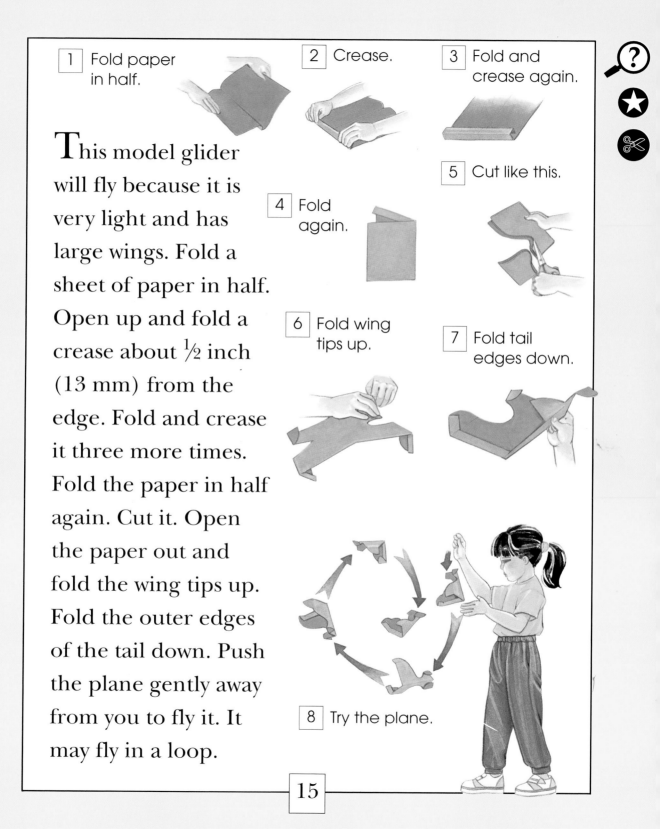

1 | Fold paper in half.

2 | Crease.

3 | Fold and crease again.

5 | Cut like this.

4 | Fold again.

This model glider will fly because it is very light and has large wings. Fold a sheet of paper in half. Open up and fold a crease about ½ inch (13 mm) from the edge. Fold and crease it three more times. Fold the paper in half again. Cut it. Open the paper out and fold the wing tips up. Fold the outer edges of the tail down. Push the plane gently away from you to fly it. It may fly in a loop.

6 | Fold wing tips up.

7 | Fold tail edges down.

8 | Try the plane.

15

# Propellers and Engines

Most airplanes have one or more engines. Sometimes each engine turns a propeller. A propeller is like a big fan. The front of the propeller blades are curved. The air behind the propeller pushes harder than the air in front of the propeller. This makes the airplane move forward. Airplanes are big and heavy. A very big push or force is needed to move an airplane. That is why airplane engines are so powerful. That is also why many airplanes have more than one engine.

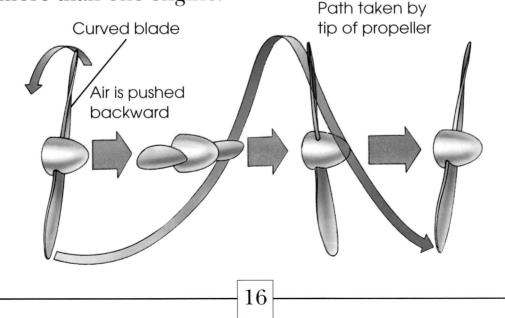

Curved blade

Path taken by tip of propeller

Air is pushed backward

When a plane is flying, four forces keep it straight and level.
These are lift, weight, thrust, and drag.

**Forces acting on airplanes**

Lift

Drag

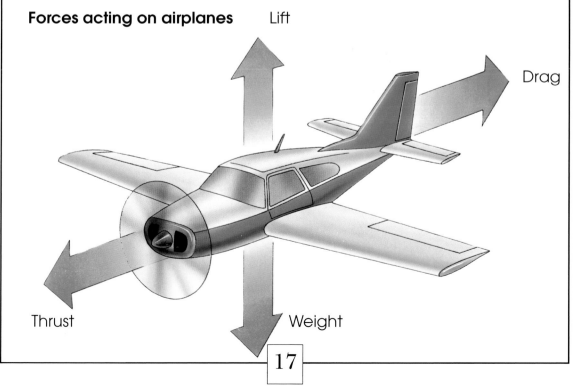

Thrust

Weight

# How an Aircraft Is Steered
## See for Yourself

An aircraft has to be able to turn. It has to be able to climb or dive. To do this, most aircraft have special flaps. These are on the wings, stabilizer, and fins. The pilot uses special controls to move the flaps.

The three main movements a plane makes have special names. They are shown here.

**Yawing**

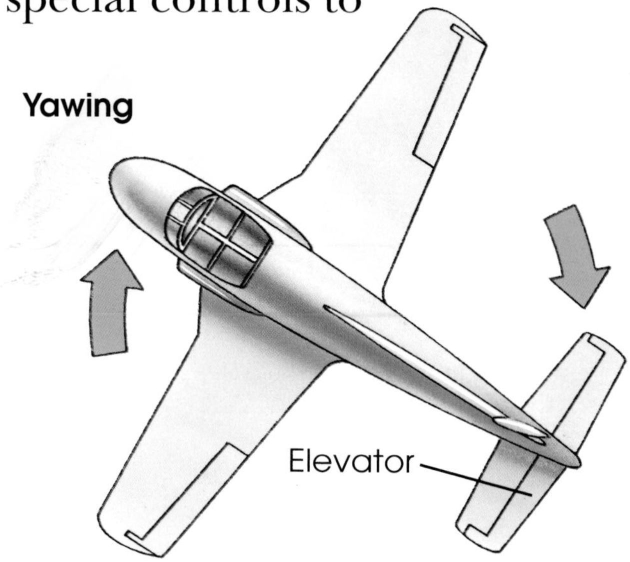

Elevator

Rudder

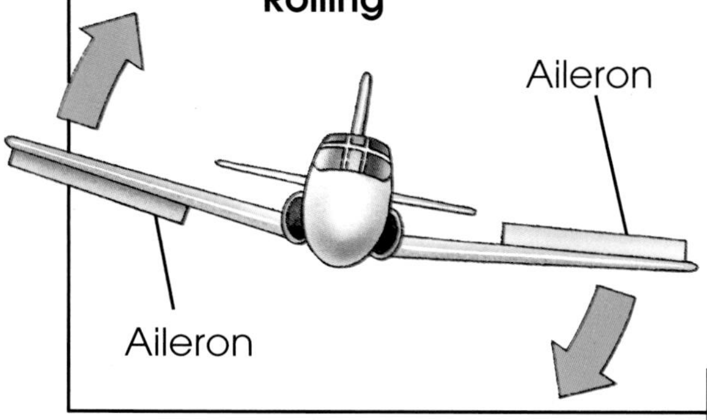

**Pitching**

**Rolling**

Aileron

Aileron

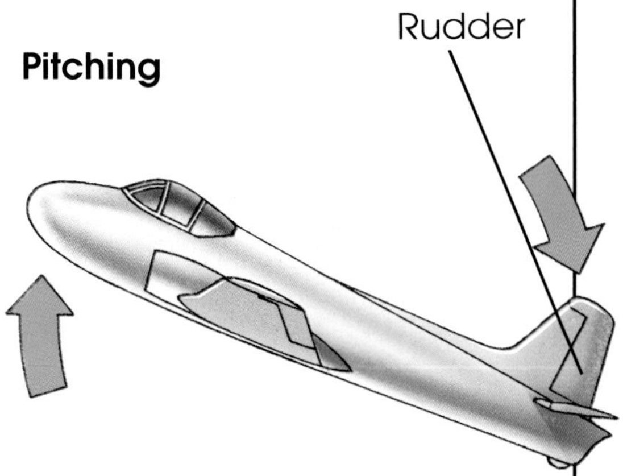

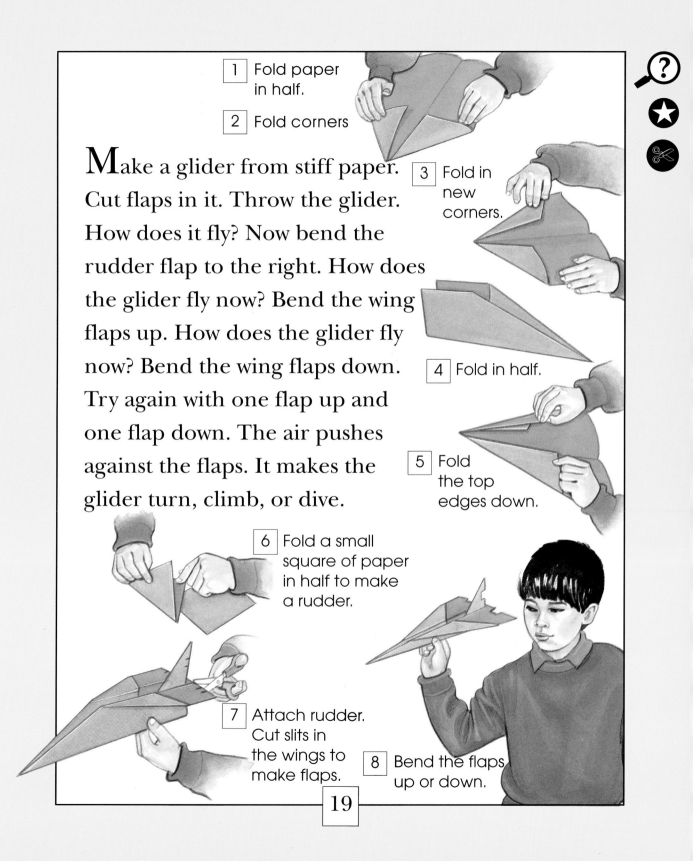

1 Fold paper in half.

2 Fold corners

Make a glider from stiff paper. Cut flaps in it. Throw the glider. How does it fly? Now bend the rudder flap to the right. How does the glider fly now? Bend the wing flaps up. How does the glider fly now? Bend the wing flaps down. Try again with one flap up and one flap down. The air pushes against the flaps. It makes the glider turn, climb, or dive.

3 Fold in new corners.

4 Fold in half.

5 Fold the top edges down.

6 Fold a small square of paper in half to make a rudder.

7 Attach rudder. Cut slits in the wings to make flaps.

8 Bend the flaps up or down.

19

A helicopter can fly straight up or down. It can hover in the air. It can fly backward, forward, or sideways. A helicopter does not have fixed wings. Instead it has rotor blades turned by an engine. The rotor blades are each shaped like a wing. When the big rotor blades spin around fast, the helicopter lifts off the ground. The tail rotor keeps the helicopter steady. It also helps to steer it.

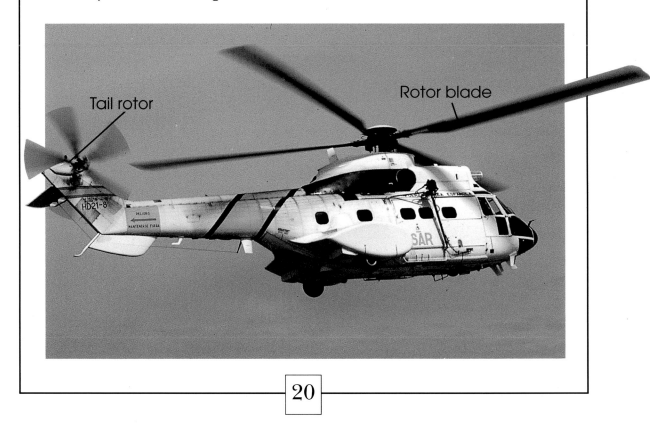

Tail rotor

Rotor blade

Paper clip

1 Cut slit

Slit

2 Fold out the wings.

3 Weight it with a paper clip.

4 Drop the rotor.

Find a piece of stiff paper, about 8 by 4 inches (21 by 11 cm). Use this to make a model helicopter rotor. Cut and fold the paper like this. Weight it with a paper clip. Drop the rotor. Watch it spiral down to the ground. How can you make a rotor that will fall very slowly? How can you make a rotor that will fall very fast?

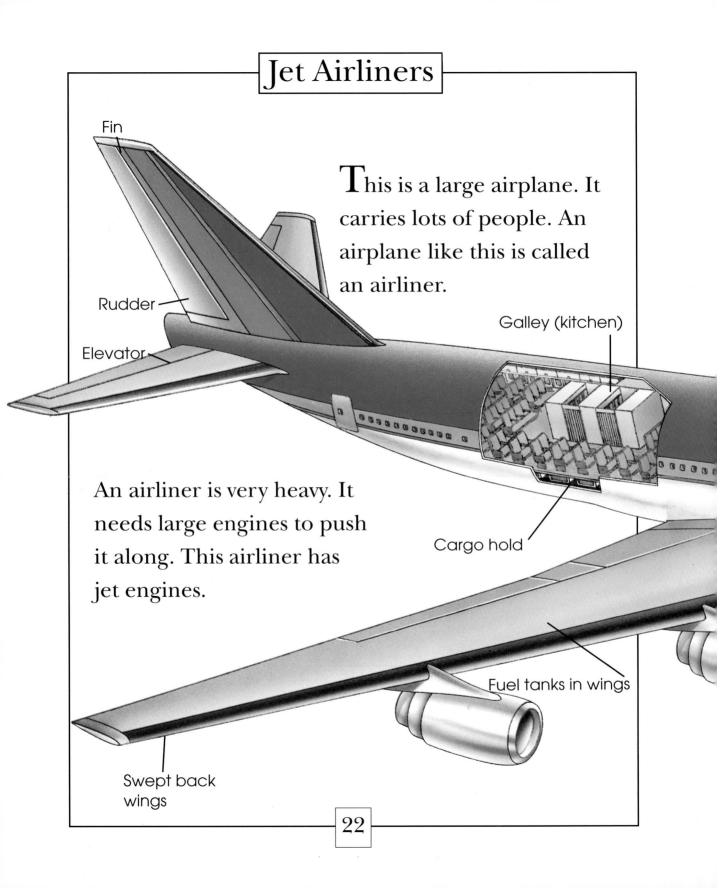

Fin

Rudder

Elevator

This is a large airplane. It carries lots of people. An airplane like this is called an airliner.

Galley (kitchen)

Cargo hold

An airliner is very heavy. It needs large engines to push it along. This airliner has jet engines.

Fuel tanks in wings

Swept back wings

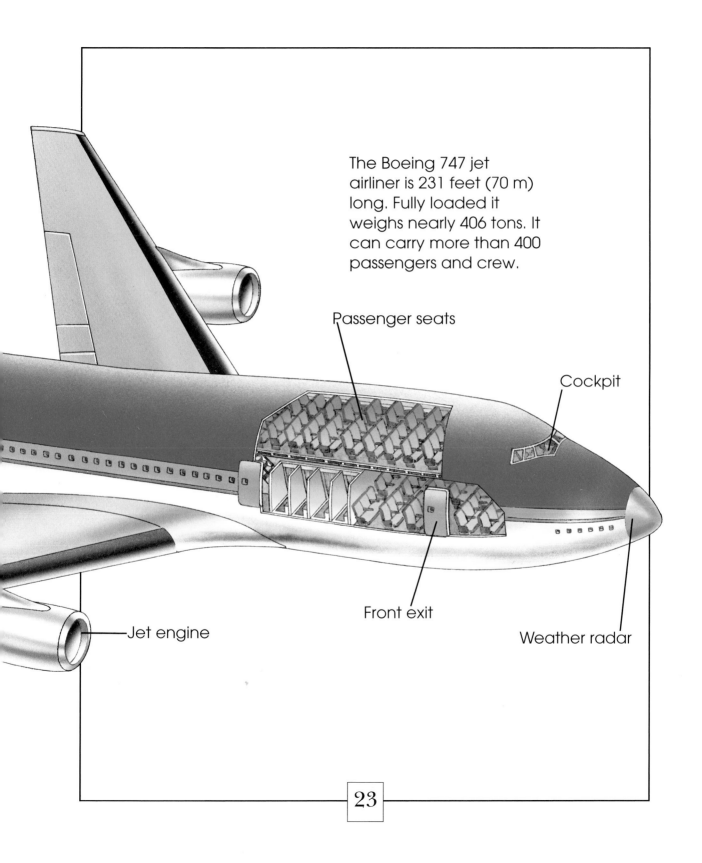

The Boeing 747 jet airliner is 231 feet (70 m) long. Fully loaded it weighs nearly 406 tons. It can carry more than 400 passengers and crew.

Passenger seats

Cockpit

Front exit

Jet engine

Weather radar

Jet engines can push an aircraft very hard. Then it can fly fast. Jet engines suck air in at the front. Inside the engine, a fuel is burned. The fuel is made from oil. The burning fuel makes lots of very hot gases.

The hot gases and air rush out of the back of the engine. They push the engine, and the aircraft, forward.

Fuel pumped in

Hot gases rush out.

Fuel and air burned

Most air goes straight through.

Some air goes through compressor, which squeezes it

Fan sucks in air

When you let go of a balloon, the air rushes out. The air rushing out of the balloon pushes it in the opposite direction. A jet engine uses this same kind of force. Hot gases rush out of the back of the engine. They push the aircraft forward.

Make a balloon jet engine. Put a strong thread through two pieces of a drinking straw. Pull it tight. Tie the ends of the thread to the backs of two chairs.

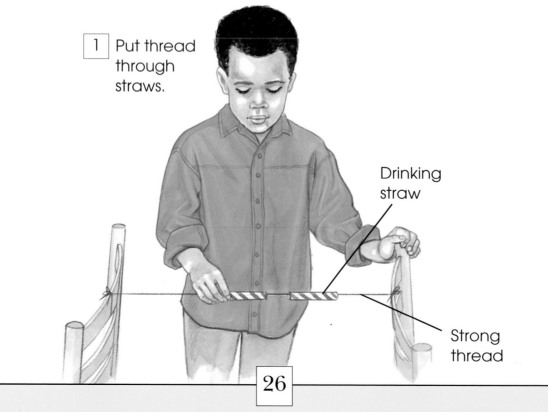

1 Put thread through straws.

Drinking straw

Strong thread

26

Blow up the balloon, and pinch it closed. Tape the drinking straws to the top of the balloon. Move the balloon to one end of the thread. Then let the balloon go. Which way does the air go? Which way does the balloon go?

3 Let go.

27

Some aircraft can fly very fast. They all have jet engines. They are also streamlined. This means they are shaped so they can slip through the air easily. Concorde is the fastest airliner. It has four jet engines. It can fly at more than 1,450 miles (2,335 km) per hour.

The Concorde flies from New York to London in about 4 hours.

Sometimes it is necessary to move slowly through the air. A parachute falls slowly through the air. Parachutes can be used to drop soldiers from an aircraft. They can be used to drop boxes of food. Pilots can escape from a damaged aircraft with a parachute. Some very fast aircraft use a parachute to slow them down when they land. Some people use a parachute for fun.

# Parachutes
## See for Yourself

Make your own model parachute. Cut out a circle from a plastic bag. Tape four pieces of long thread to the circle. Tie a small toy or thread spool to the ends. Throw the parachute into the air. Watch how the parachute fills with air. Air pushes up under the parachute so it falls slowly. Try this with a slightly heavier toy. Does it fall faster or slower?

Plastic bag

1 Cut out circle.

2 Tape string.

3 Tie the toy.

4 Let go.

# Glossary

**Air** The mixture of gases that surrounds the Earth, and that we breathe.

**Aircraft** Any flying machine, with or without an engine.

**Airfoil** Any surface, like an aircraft wing, which is shaped to produce lift when air flows past it.

**Airliner** A large passenger-carrying aircraft.

**Drag** The force of the air pushing against an aircraft.

**Flap** One of the hinged surfaces on the wings or stabilizer of an aircraft.

**Force** A push or pull. A force can start or stop something moving, change its direction, or change its shape.

**Fuel** A material that is burned to produce heat or power. Coal, oil, wood, and gasoline are fuels.

**Gas** Any substance that, like air, expands to completely fill a container.

**Glider** A kind of aircraft without an engine.

**Jet engine** An engine that drives an aircraft or vehicle by sending out a powerful jet of gases.

**Lift** The force caused by air moving at different speeds above and below an aircraft's wings. Lift keeps the aircraft in flight.

**Parachute** An umbrella-shaped device used for dropping safely from an aircraft.

**Propeller** A type of fan that turns rapidly to drive an aircraft along.

**Rotor** The large propeller on top of a helicopter.

**Streamlining** The design of an aircraft so that it slips smoothly and easily through the air.

**Thermal** A column of warm air rising from the ground.

**Thrust** The force that pulls an aircraft forward.

# Index

# DATE DUE

| | | | |
|---|---|---|---|
| | | | |
| | | | |
| | | | |
| | | | |
| | | | |
| | | | |
| | | | |
| | | | |
| | | | |
| | | | |
| | | | |
| | | | |
| | | | |